COVER PHOTO
ANITA VAN DER BILT

GREAT THANKS TO MANY FRIENDS

© 2018 Luka van den Driesschen - Spirit on Sound
ISBN 978-90-817056-3-9

All rights reserved. No part of this book may be reproduced, stored in a retrieval system or transmitted in any form or by any means without the prior written permission of the publishers, except by a reviewer who may quote brief passages in a review to be printed in a newspaper, magazine or journal.

Painting by Sanjeev Sharma India

TRILOGIE
LUKA VAN DEN DRIESSCHEN

SINGER OF LIGHT

To BE OR NOT TO BE

That's Not The Question

Spiritual Aphorisms

by Luka van den Driesschen

This is the song I sing for you
It is the sound of creation
In endless flow
Given to us all
When our heart is open
And our ears are silent

Between breaths
We can see and hear
This silence
That tells us
Who we are

Then we'll learn
We are no one
No one
To know

I once had a dream:
In truth we find
All we are
And all we are not

Being is seeing
It's me, who calls you
And you, who's calling me
We hear each other
In one sound, one song
The song of love

Being in silence
We are all one

*If we don't fill our spaces with love
Others will fill them with hate*

*Men of tomorrow
Can not be understood today*

*Like the sky and the earth
Like the sun and the moon
Stars are the seeds of light
Twinkling in our hearts*

*The beggar will become a king
And the king becomes a beggar*

We find existence in creation

*Flowers can't explain
How to be a flower*

*In death you go
Beyond your ego*

Words dance on silence
Songs fly above words

You don't know who you are
If you really did
You wouldn't know

I am an outsider to myself
Looking inward

Only timelessness
Can make a flower bloom

In all illusion
One dream stays alive:
To come home and awake

Only in lonesomeness
You meet your true self

Amazing how great you are

When you feel so small

Not that I fit into the world
But the world fits into me

Light can blind your eyes

Darkness can blind your soul

Truth can not be found
It reveals itself

The tree of wisdom shows
There is nothing new

You only look for God
When you can't find him
While he's everywhere

Artists are the teachers
Of tomorrow
Suffering today

We can only stand up
When we have fallen

One loses
If one takes
More
Than one can give

*One of the greatest lessons of life
Is to learn not to judge*

*When you hold on to yourself
What's the need of holding on to others ?*

*Some things are only certain
When they are uncertain*

You find your soul in emptiness

Look inside your heart
Its beat is your song
On which you can dance
Your way to nowhere

We do our utmost
To avoid
Finding ourselves

When growth is endless
How can you be someone?

Money gives you more power
To be more miserable

Know your shadow
And you know yourself

Words is just one way

*Come weary traveller
Unpack your bags
And see for yourself
That all
You are carrying with you
Is yourself*

*When we understand
That death can awaken our soul
We will never be afraid again*

Leaving home
Can bring you home;
Just leaving home
Won't

Drifting on the wind is scaring
Letting the child drift in you,
daring

The moon is always with us
But we are not always with the
moon

In light
There are no hiding places

Like you breathe
Just let it happen

The fear of light
Blinds our ego

Insight is out sight
Looking in
Is looking out

No matter
You are a star

When our inner child is hurt
It hurts our growth

If we could see
We are standing on ourselves
We would move aside

Brick by brick
We build our wall
Brick by brick
We need to tear it down

Think of nothing
And you will be filled

*Reach out to nowhere
And you 'll be there*

*The first sound we make
Is a cry:
Laughter comes after*

*I am not the poet
The poet is me*

You are never angry with me
Only with yourself

When you find joy
Don't hold on to it

We live with need and greed
Because we have too much

A dreamer looks up
An awakened spirit
Look around

In wisdom
You find truth
By wondering
You find wonders

Standing on top
You can't see
Your own mountain

Blindness
Opens your heart
To darkness

When the mystic speaks
It is not the truth

When you are astray
You are on your way

Don't look for existence
For it has already found you

Grow young
Grow wild
Grow up
To be a child

He who locks the other away
Is still looking for his own key

The road to nowhere
Is nowhere

We hide
Not to be hurt

Hiding hurts
When we hide
Not to be hurt

To close doors
You must be open

Rivers don't smell
Because they flow

Normality is often
The fear of being yourself

*Sometimes
You have to be blind
To see*

*Go
With your own flow*

*The greatest gift
Is to forgive
Yourself*

*mind is hell
Your heart
The key to your soul*

*Life is like flying:
You have to let go*

*The mind is the projector;
Our lives
The film being played*

*We can only be aware
Of our awareness
When we are aware*

*Meditation by creation,
Creation by meditation*

*We are all asleep
Not aware
Of who we are*

*Close your eyes
And you can see all*

*We leave our shore of birth
And step into the world
In search for the ocean
We just left behind*

*In the mirror of life
We can see our true face:
The face of purity
The pearl of living*

*The highest form of living
Is love*

*We are the pearl
Hidden in our own shell*

*Pour joy into the world
And the world
Will smile back to you*

*A man is only stupid
When he refuses to learn
From being stupid*

*The journey itself
Is our destination*

*Someone whose heart is a rose
Must feel the thorns now and then*

*No one can lead you astray
When you know yourself*

Be a watcher
Keep watching yourself

Recondition your eyes
To the eyes of a child

Let all be it
And all will be

The secret of life is transformation

Our journey is within;
If we had to travel far
God would have
Given us wings

We cannot find ourselves
By only following others

*Whatever you see in others
Is alive in you*

*Every note sung
Holds the breath of existence*

*Work not to work
Work not to live
Work in love
With your work*

Live not to live
Live in love with life

Often we listen to others
Only because we don't understand
What our own heart is saying

Only in true freedom
We find ourselves

*It's always the other,
Who seems wrong,
That doesn't make it right*

*You can only be a light
When there is darkness
Around you*

*Just like the earth you can turn,
Just like the stars, you can shine*

People keep asking questions,
While we all know the answers

Sometimes we are
Too blind to see
How beautiful we are

Space is so endless
There is not even
A beginning

No one rules the world,
Only creation is creating

If we all had nothing to say
We would meet in depth

Words keep us apart

The moment we create,
We are living in creation

We are no more
And no less
Than we are

We can only let others be
Who they are
When we let ourselves be
Who we are

Creation is our destination

Money is only good
When it gives you freedom

No one, but no None
Can give you happiness

The world has become so noisy
That we no longer hear ourselves

The art of living
Is finding something new
In something old

The mind always wants to be there

In death we hold on to nothing

People are crazy
To think they are not crazy

You belong to nobody
But yourself

You see me as you are

We often turn back
Out of fear of growing

No matter how many roads
You walk down in life
In the end they all lead back
To yourself

I can only touch in you
What I can touch in me

The meaning of life
Is transformation

Give light to yourself
And darkness will disappear

*We are responsible
Not for what we are,
But for what have become*

*Our inner worth
Is worth more
Than the sum
Of all our possessions*

*You don't need a ticket
To start your inner journey
Today*

Truth is speechless

The moment is this
Never that

We live outside ourselves

*Man's true face
Is like the hidden seed
Of a flower*

*About light
No one can speak
Or write*

*A happy person
Always stands alone*

*Accept all that you are
And you will accept others*

*Every morning
Is the beginning
Of a new night*

*All that holds a seed
Holds a flower*

Allow a child to teach you
And you'll become
A great teacher

Life is learning
Not to learn

You lose your freedom
In identification

Our judgement s on others
Are often our own shortcomings

We always wait for nothing

Every pearl hides a teardrop

You look for me
To find yourself
And when you have found
Others will start
Looking for you

There must be dreamers
For others to awake

A true vision
Is without ambition

*All the time
I say the same thing:
Come to yourself*

*We are no longer the person
We were one moment ago*

*Remove the old from your eyes
And the world will look like new*

We are old souls
In search
Of what was always there

You need the other
To tell you what to do,
The moment you stop listening
To your own heart

A wise man is without words

Rain holds the secret of growth
Thunder holds the secret of lightning

Darkness hides our shadow
Find your shadow,
And you know
Who you are

Inside you
There is a mountain
You can climb

To all the down and out:
Where there is a way down,
There 's a way out

All goes so much faster
When we live without time

Home is
Where we are

*The person
We are most afraid of
To meet
Is our self*

*Only one touch of light
Can transform our life forever*

*Create
Only for the sake
Of creation*

The body may grow old
But the rest is timeless

You will never be poor
If you allow existence
To give

I found you in me
And me in you

*Nature gives herself to you
But do you give yourself to nature
?*

*The only barrier to yourself
Is your own ego*

*The mind believes
The heart knows*

*The heart is
The only gate to paradise*

Fear is the killer of growth

*We only cry out of loneliness
When we miss ourselves*

There is only one way
And that is yours

The more you see yourself
The more you see the other

You can only taste the sweetness of life
When you have tasted the bitterness first

*Life doesn't know failures
Only we do*

*True wisdom
Knows nothing*

*There is no destination
Only creation*

I write so I can sing
And sing so I can write

When all longing comes to an end
The seed of love starts to grow

In death lie all the answers
But who wants to know ?

I want to write
About you
But how come
It's always me
I write about

Some people find paradise in hell

We are born with a golden thread
To sew the pieces of life together
To become
Whole again

Streams of tears
Make room for laughter

If you can be grateful
For what you don't have
You created a miracle
To yourself

I am such a greedy man
Wanting nothing

Dance and you will fly
Sing and you 'll find harmony

Never I have heard a tree say
Give me back my apple

Listening to the song of a bird
Makes your heart sing too

The earth has no boundaries
Only we have

like our eyes are
The mirror of our soul,
The soul is the mirror
Of our existence

Truth spoken
Is only a reflection
Of truth

*Inspiration comes
From doing nothing*

*Relax
We are only born to die*

*Love has no name
It 's simply there*

In nothing
We find all

In everything
Grows a seed of love

When you think you are worthless
You have nothing to share

We are all diamonds
Reflecting the light
Of each other

Don't look ahead
Just leave your head
Where it is

You are not alone
You only think you are

*The gift of song
Lives in the heart
Of all people*

*People make life complicated
Because it is too simple*

*When people say
There is no problem
You can be sure
There is one*

Darkness
Reminds us of
Light

Love is like a burning fire
Be careful
You might get hurt

Be grateful for everything
And you will be blessed with joy

*Look down at the earth
Before you look at the sky*

*We run far
To find home
And when we found it
We keep running*

*The wind plays softly with the trees
Or do the trees play softly with the wind?*

Heaven is on earth
That's why we can not find it

The best way to get drunk
Is to fill yourself up
With existence

Finding existence
Is like drinking
From an empty bottle

The God we project
Is neither
Dead or alive

We simply have to die
To be born again

Paradise lies at our feet
That's why we can't find it

*The tree of wisdom
Stands in paradise*

*We often kick ourselves
And then start screaming
That we are hurt*

The road to wisdom is endless

Only if we live without need
We can share without greed

You tasted the honey
You tasted the wine
Why not taste the divine ?

We live together
On one little planet
And all we do
Is destroy it

Fear is
The basic ingredient
Of all greed

Only a happy person
Can flow
And grow
Into a flower

We are born asleep
One day to awake

*It's much easier
To open up your eyes
In darkness*

*We fail to keep our children
children*

*If we can accept
Everything
In complete surrender
We can live in peace
And harmony
In total splendor*

*Everything passes
Nothing is here to stay*

*I have so much
For you have so little
You have so much
For I have so little*

Life is ordinary

Death means: nothing

Growth is everywhere:
Inside and
Outside

Loneliness is one minus one

The moment we separate
We are lost

Truth comes out of nothing

Poverty in wisdom
Is the most serious of all

Every moment we live
A moment dies

People hurry to die

Life gives you
A taste of everything

What is truth ?
Just a reflection
Of your being

It's the mind
That drives you crazy
Never the heart

Growing in love
Does not feel like falling

Our mind
Always sings
An old song

Living is leaving the past,
Accepting the moment

The sun shines every day

*When the mind is silent,
The heart starts singing*

*You don't have to be holy
To become whole*

*Without depth
No height*

Even a diamond
Can not sparkle
In darkness

No one can change your life
But you

To be or not to be
That's not the question

The richer the heart,
The poorer the mind

Our mind
Created time

Darkness fights
Against the light;
It's not the light
Fighting against darkness

Beyond every horizon
Lies another one

You are so unique
But you fail to see it

Come and dance in the sun
It shines for everyone

*Tears show you depth
Love shows you height*

Let someone love you

*We are all students,
The universe
Our university*

*It's impossible
To love tomorrow*

*No one can give you
Your freedom*

*You can only find the light
Inside yourself*

All ripe fruits
Fall from the tree

Peace never comes
It is and was always there

Only by thinking
We make mistakes

The answer is no answer

Love has no colour

Mothers with children
Are children with mothers

So much is given
If we don't ask

Only when you lose yourself
You can find it

The only one we can understand
Is our self

Only because you feel poor
You want to be rich

Our greed is our own emptiness

The whole universe lives in you

You're free
When you say so

I have come into your life
Because you have come into mine

We project into the world
What we think we are

The whole world
Is a playground
For lovers
For children;
To others
It's a work yard,
To many
A battlefield

Dropping out is
Dropping in

Not knowing is growing

Traveling will never bring you home

*We are all on the way
To love or hate*

*Before every word is said,
There is silence*

*The problem is
That there is no problem*

*A tree doesn't need
To move
To grow*

*We can't walk
Without leaving
Footprints in the sand*

Nature is beautiful
You are nature

All you need is
Meditation,
Not medication

You are the world,
We are the world

Our true authentic face
Is our creation

You can't force
A flower to grow

Only thinking
Can drive you crazy

*The water of the river
Knows only one way
To reach the ocean*

Listen to the silence of a stone

*When you know how to die,
You know how to live*

The greatest wonder of all
Is you

All great men are dreamers

The greatest gift is love

We hold so many keys
To so many doors

Only creation gives birth
To something new

Growth:
Two steps forward
One step backwards

Until one finds
One's inner flower
Everyone is crazy

Only a way further
There is no way back

May words
Become light
In you

When you can laugh
Because you've lost
You're a winner

Wisdom is seeing the difference
Until the difference is gone

True power comes from the heart

*Your thoughts
Are not yours*

*Death is also
A state of being*

*Life is full of critics
And the most critical
Is you*

We are the prisoners
Of our own thoughts
And emotions

You can look at the stars
And break a leg
At the same time

Creation can only be
In the moment

We think we love,
That's the problem

We need love
For we are not love

Only knowing
That we don't know
Is real knowing

*Sometimes
We are so
Filled with joy
That it makes us
Feel sorry*

*Love is not blind,
We are*

*Only mankind can give birth
To paradise on earth*

What is alive in me,
Is alive in you

Love is always in the moment

No door is closed
Until we say so

To improve your condition:
Drop all your conditions

You don't need another light
When you are switched on

Grow up
Be a child

You can only see me
Through your eyes

To find the way
Follow your own footsteps

We remain in darkness
Because it's feels familiar

A seed is born out of a seed

*A thing is perfect
When it's not*

*We are standing
In the middle
Of our selves*

Our mind blocks our being

We can believe anything
And know nothing

Reject
And you'll be rejected

*Pain can be
The beginning of joy*

The singer leaves his song behind

*Growth comes in spirals
Not in circles*

*The Gods are angry
When we are*

*You are born
To give birth
To yourself*

*Our minds keeps
Our heart gives*

*No tree can grow
Without roots*

When there is no ego
There is only you

I could not have done better
Than I did
But I can do better

We think we cry
For our beloved ones
Not knowing
We are crying
For ourselves

*And the mystic turned around
And spoke
His last words to the tree*

*Since I have known you,
He said,
I have seen you grow tall
And your roots
Have grown deeper
To the depths of the earth*

*I also have seen,
He said,
Your flowers,
Bright as the sun*

*Thank you,
Said the mystic,
For reflecting
My inner being.
Together
We have become one*

Now I'll be on my way
Wider and further

In endless time.
You,
Said the mystic,
Were my wisdom,
My growth,
My shade in the sun,
My resting place
When my eyes were heavy

Now my eyes are open
And I see you
Standing there
In all your lonesomeness.

I see you as you are
I see me as I am
I see you as I am

PHOTO LUKA

Santorini
GODDESS OF PERISSA

ATLANTIS IS CALLING

Spiritual
Words And
Photos
from the
Island Of
Santorini
by

LUKA VAN DEN DRIESSCHEN

SINGER OF LIGHT

In the year 1986, after an odyssey of more than thirty years, destiny had brought me to the Greek island of Santorini. This volcanic island in the middle of the Aegean Sea, has always been surrounded by myths and spiritual energy. It's been said that a big explosion of the volcano on the island approximately 1500 B.C should have caused the drowning of Atlantis. Mankind has been searching for hundreds of years to find this lost island again. Until now they found ruins only.
But while archaeologists keep searching, there is another Atlantis, the continent of our soul, that can be found. If only one starts listening again with the heart and looks beyond. When one starts to realize that we are not our feelings nor our thoughts.

For three months I was part of the mountains, the sea and the people of Santorini. It was In Perissa, that Santorini spoke to me in silence. I called this inner voice the GODDESS OF ATLANTIS. I want to share with you these spiritual words of wisdom and eternal light. These silent songs, that sounded inside of me so many years ago, can now be heard by all of you. Just lend me your ears and follow your heart to your own destination. Atlantis is calling!

Luka van den Driesschen, 2018

Atlantis stream flows in the hearts of the people Atlantis dream is awake in everyone's heart

Perissa in Greek means whole The vertical of the Mountains And the horizontal of the Beach

It is our destination to become whole To come home.

Song of my heart
You dropped in silence
Starless sky
You are
empty
Growing
flower
You have
disappeared
Emptiness is taking
over Nothing is
entering Even
entering is fading
Only the sound of the harp
remains Playing the tune
Over and over again
It's a song from
heaven Sounding
through me Silently
Like a sky-less
sky Only heart
From the
depth Of
Santorini

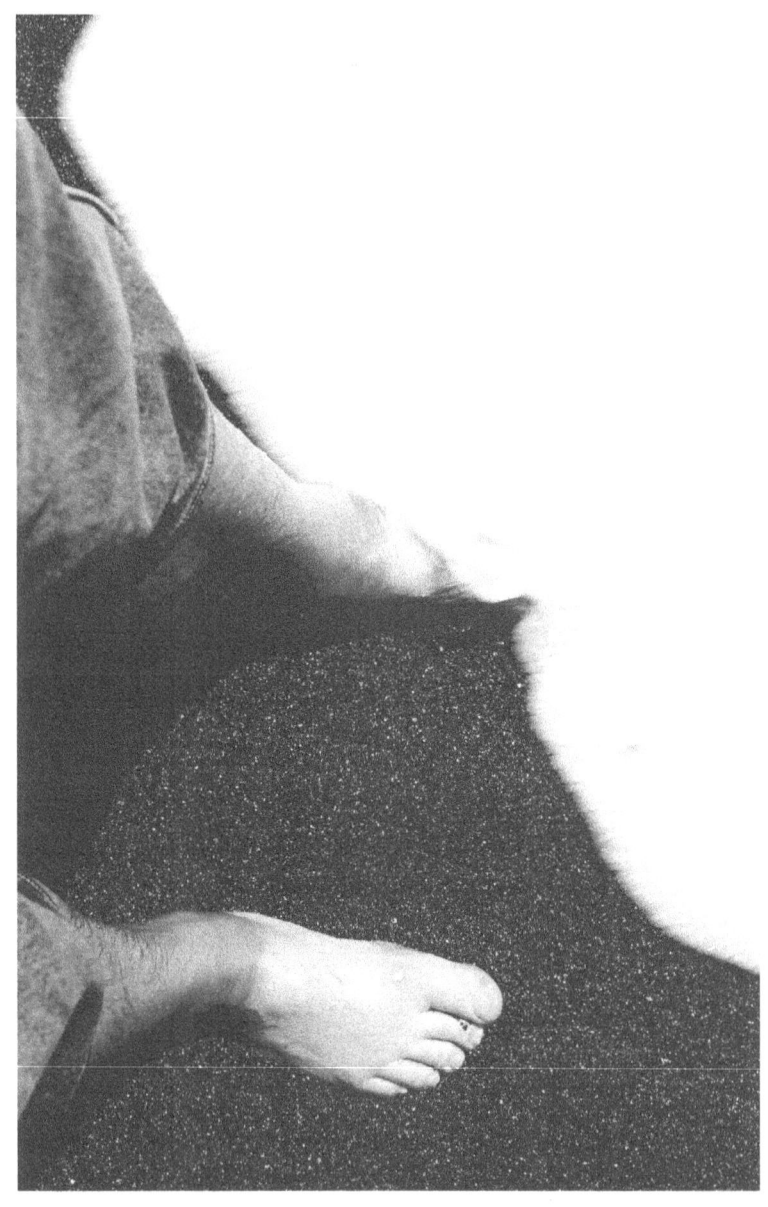

*Goddess of ATLANTIS, Goddess of the
Sea... Speak to me of the sea.*

The sea is to be.

*It has no compass, no direction,
no grip So that you are drifting on
the wind.
And it is the wind that takes you to your
destination. Like the seed of a flower touched to
go and grow. And so it is with you, dear
friends:
Flow only with the wind in
you, Follow your river.
Only then you can feel peace in your
heart. Let go
For the wind, your river, knows your
destination.*

Goddess, speak to me of God.

*First you have to know there is no God to know
God All your knowledge of the past, for
knowledge is only past,
Must melt like snow before the
sun, For knowledge is only past
Then - only then - you will find
God. And when you have found
him
You will know that all is
God And that God is all.*

Goddess, can you speak once more about the sea?

*The sea has mountains which you cannot
climb. It has waters in which you can
drown.
But you cannot swim forever when someone drops
you off
in the middle of the ocean.
Nor can you walk for long on the mountains
beneath the sea.
Without drowning.
But you must drown in life to find love.
And this is what really happens when
you die. You drown to be saved
To be saved by the sea of loving light*

Goddess, can you speak to me of the mountains?

Some mountains are
high Some are low
But no mountain can be high and low
No caterpillar can be a butterfly at the same
time And it is when you see this
that you can climb every
mountain. You my friend walk
vertically
you my friend die
horizontally when both
lines meet
it becomes a cross
it's the wholeness of life one with all.

Goddess, can you speak to me of the flowers in the field?

*You can only see the flowers
when you can see your own
flower Flowers are a reflection
of what is alive in
you. But often it is
so
that you, my friend, are
asleep. And in your deep
sleep
you do not see your own
flower. become awake
and it will shine
even in the darkest night. So that you'll never be
lost. It's like your own star watching over you.
Twinkling in your heart being the flower you are.*

Goddess, can you show me the stars?

*I cannot show you
anything it is only you
that can see.
Some people that are colour-
blind see a yellow rose
and maybe you see a red one.
Some people see only money in
life you may see only greed.
Others are searching always
searching always on the way,
going past things not being it, not
seeing it.
So how can I show you the stars.
Be a star and you outshine them
all.*

*Goddess, can you speak to me about man and
woman, woman and man?*

*Man and woman are
searching always searching
to find themselves.
They keep thinking unconsciously that they are
lost
but they are not lost at
all. They only think
they are.
And it is when these thoughts are
dropped that you will find.
Dolphins do not
ask am I a
dolphin?
A flower does not
ask am I a flower?
Even the mountains are silent
during the day as well as the
night. Being is seeing
So why keep on
searching Just be like
the mountains, the
flowers and the sea.
For you are all of these.*

Goddess, you have spoken so much, tell me: where do your words come from?

*The words you
hear are not from
me but from you.
You are hearing them.
It is your own inner voice that sings.
It is the silence of your truth that
sounds. It is the Goddess in your soul
that whisper, not me. If a player plays
his flute and there is no one to listen. ?
Then he is the only one who can
hear. And so it is with these
words.
Only you can hear your own sound.
And never can anyone hear it like you
do.*

*Oh Goddess, just before you go to
sleep tell me one more story...
I have no more questions.*

*Why another story
when there are no more questions.
The fact that you ask me,
suggests that you still
have For if you really did
not have, Your heart
would be silent. And it is
only in silence
that you will know all.
But first we have
questions, always
questions.
And it is good only good
when all questioning has
stopped.
For then you start knowing all by
yourself. For all wisdom is in you.
Only in you.
Never in a
book. Never.*

Goddess, can you tell me about Tomorrow?

*Never there will be a
tomorrow Because tomorrow
never comes. But all life goes
on
That is why people often
think that there is a
tomorrow.
But life itself
changes. You
change
every thousandth of a
second. You grow and die
every breath is death
unknowing like a
flower. Your face
directed towards the
sun Unless you turn
your head away.
But will the flower still be growing
tomorrow? The bird still flying?
The bird may sit still and the flower may
have dropped its flower. But the flower
still exists, the bird still exists, Even if
they have died.
So there is no tomorrow – only your
tomorrow According to your
expectations..*

*While all keeps on
flowering and showering*

*But Goddess of the Sea, and how about
Yesterday ?*

*Yesterday is a reflection of the
past only a reflection.
It is not there and never was.
If the sun was shining yesterday
and today the sun has gone behind a
cloud can you feel or see the sun?
Yes, you can still see the
sun, But only in your
dreams,
in your imagination. .
Yesterday is gone,
melted and dissolved in the present Yesterday
never was
and never is.
There is only
This, And only
This.*

*Goddess, will you never leave me
alone?*

*Your fear to be alone
is a common human
fear.
It's the fear of being yourself.
And it is only when you see yourself
that you have found yourself.
But always we try to hold on to the
fear for that's what we know.*

Goddess, when man landed on the moon - was that of great importance?

It was and it was
not. It was
important,
because for the very first time in human
existence Man had reached the moon.
They reached, but did not really
touch it. Not with their soul.
It is only when you touch the moon with your
soul that you become whole.
Whole with the stars and the sun
Absorbed in the eternal circle of
twilight in being!

*Goddess, can you speak to me about
children?*

*Children are born
innocent. We corrupt
them
for we have been children
and have been corrupted
too.
So our parents have been children and
were corrupted.
To find back our authentic selves,
we grown-ups have to be born
again. To dance to laugh to sing to
be free. To be open like the net of a
fisherman where the wind can
blow through. When we all are
reborn
the priests,
politicians our
teachers at school
we will understand
the nature of being.
The playful inner
child That we all
are*

*Goddess, when I die will I then see
you?*

*You will see me for you will see
yourself. And it is only when you see
yourself that you will see me.
Most people are afraid to die
They want to hold on, stay attached.
And I am saying
only when you let
go you will flow.
Cause when you hold on
to the sides of the river
Soon your hands will
cramp your arms will
become tired. And so you
live your life, always in a
cramp.
Until you let go
then you flow.
Carried by the
river seeing
yourself,
in the crystal clear
mirror of your
authentic face.*

*Goddess of, Santorini, of
Atlantis... Can I see more than I
am seeing now?*

*How much are you
seeing? Ask yourself this
question
how much are you really
seeing? To see all,
Like the yin and the
yang, your left must
melt
with your right.
So they become one.
And when the two become
one Then there is three.
And this is called your third
eye. Only then you can look
beyond and see
there is no beyond.
Then you can see all there is and
was
Now and always.*

*Goddess, I have named you
this for I feel you are not
God.
But where is he?*

*He is in me, God is in the Goddess
And only when God meets the Goddess There is
God.
A woman also has the heart of a
man. And a man the heart of a
woman. But we rebel.
We have to become the
sun and the moon
together.
We rebel cause that is how we are being brought
up. Only when we accept the woman in the man
and the man in the
woman we will you
meet Godliness.
That's why men keep chasing
women. To find themselves.
They keep on chasing
women. But never meet
their woman that lives
inside of them.
We all
misunderstand. until
we have found our
own woman or man
breathing inside our souls*

Goddess of my soul,

*I am beginning to understand
something.
The fact that you understand,
proofs that you do not see.
I want you to understand
nothing, Only to see.
For seeing is being.
Real listening has no ears, no mind.
Real listening goes like the wind that
blows through the trees.
The leaves are shaking
The branches bend a
little
and the trunk stands firmly in the
ground. While the wind blows free.
And then you are. Then you really
see. Then you see what you are. Who
you are. And always was.*

*Goddess, can you give me
something One more time?
I don't know what...*

*What you do not
know you can give to
yourself.
It is the greatest present of
life. I cannot give you this.
You can only give this to yourself.
Only when you have given it to
yourself, You can share it with
others.
Only then.
And one more time does not exist.
A flower does not flower one more
time and then no more.
It keeps spreading its
fragrance On and on,
invisibly.
So give yourself all there is to
give. And you will be giving
always.*

Goddess, are you not a bit too serious?

*Let me tell you a
joke. The joke is me.
But not many see it.
All the time I am telling you the greatest joke of all.
And the laughter comes from deep down So very deep…
But you miss
it. The joke is
me. The joke
is you.
So if you are taking me
serious you are taking
yourself serious I really
enjoy myself.
For the greatest joke are
we. Life is a play, like a
child. And when your
laughter can fill the whole
valley
you have reached
the mountaintop.*

Goddess, are you a danger to the world?

*Yes and no
and so are
you.
For tell me: is a flower a
danger? Is a bird a danger?
Is love dangerous?
Ask yourself these questions And
danger will speak to you.
And then you will know the
answer. Dropping the ego
looking into
yourself is full of
fear.
For to fly so high
one must reach for the sky and leave
the earth behind (Pure light can
burn your eyes Pure love melts the
ego)*

*Goddess, why do you call yourself
Goddess, while you are you and me is
me?*

*I want you to feel your own
Goddess When you touch that
word,
you will become silent.
For you are you and not your name.
Cause when you have become a name
any name,
you will have lost your
you. So to find back
yourself, Become a
Goddess
And start breathing like
one. The sun is not the
sun.
The moon is not the
moon. And you are not
your name. For you are
a Goddess.
Until you are no more.*

Goddess, tell me about Greece.

Once you have tasted the inner
silence you come to Greece again
and again. Like a flower seeking
the sun or rain.
Some find it in the mountains, or by the
sea Others at the fountains of Delphi
or in the dance of the
Zorba. It's all to be found
in Greece.
Every stone on the island holds the wisdom of
being Even the tiniest grain of sand
From Perissa beach, that you hold in your
hand

Goddess, can you tell me about love?

You do not know real love.
For if you did you would not ask.
Are you a flower when you look at
it? Are you the mountains or the
sea when You see them?
You have compassion for the
other and that is beautiful.
You feel love, but are you love ?
Be love and you will have
everything Then there's no more for
you to wish. Love is the light
Love is such a
fullness. It is the
seed in you ready to
flower.
And when you are
love, Love is you.

Goddess, can nature really speak to us?

Yes and no.
Nature does not speak like you with your tongue.
But it radiates its
energies To send the
message to you And you
can read the signs For
when it's cold
when it's
hot you
know.
And when the earth
trembles or the wind
blows.
you know.
And yet it is invisible
So it is with everything around
us You can hear the very song of
loving when your heart is open
And your eyes are clear to
see. Nature sings only one
song With the sound of your
soul.

Goddess, tell me about the devil: does he exist?

You exist, so the devil exists. Hear what I am saying.
You exist, so the devil exists. You have created him
It is you in temptation
Of your inner aggression It's a
picture of the mind.
And you fight with your Devil It's Your Devil, Your fight, Your war. That is why men down the ages Have killed and made many wars. Not knowing they were only fighting with themselves.
And it is only when you stop Fighting with yourself
You will see this foolishness that no Devil can ever exist. You have created the Devil Your own aggression Transform your hate into love
And love will burn the Devil in you.

*Goddess, can you speak to me of
Santorini?*

*Of Santorini I cannot
speak It speaks to you in
silence
In your silence you will know
Santorini. Start listening to her
oceans
feel the depth of her
seas become her beauty
and you will know
Santorini And by
knowing Santorini You
will know yourself
I saw a beautiful flower
Busy growing in the black lava sand It
had no colour
it did not even smell
It was not even a flower it was me.*

Goddess,

*I am about to leave your island, but I feel so
sad. I try to hold on to your pebbles on the
beach like a baby sucking his mothers
breast.
Not wanting to let go.
You have been touched this
time. You really have been
touched
By the tremendous beauty of Santorini
And no one wants to let go of his
paradise. But the fact that you cling to
Santorini Knowing that you are going
Makes you sad
It is the same in every relationship.
And you have a wonderful relationship with
Santorini. The moment you cling
You become sad and
afraid But let me tell
you
It is your own
beauty That you
have seen. Your
own moon, Your
own stars, Your
own sea.
And when you were climbing the
mountains, You were in fact climbing
yourself.
So how can you leave me?*

*When you make love to a
woman, you make love with
yourself.
But we never realize
this. We become
possessive, We wear a
ring to cling. You hold
my pebbles and it's
only
when you let go of
these that Santorini
will live in your heart
wherever you are.
Do not try to be Santorini. It is
you.
The black lava
sand you walk on
is you. The Greek music and
wine all is you.
You taste it. You feel it.*

Goddess ,

can you shine one more light on me?

Yes, I can shine a light on you. This is what priests have done for thousands of years.
They shined the light
But they also tried to be your light But how can they ever be the light of someone else ?
You are your own light, your own star I can never be your light.
I can never be your truth
Be your own light, then you will see The light inside you and me.

Goddess of Santorini,

When I truly want to see a flower
I feel a fear rising. Can you tell me why?

The flower is you.
Love is the seed and you are the flower.
When we feel a rose or a lotus-flower with open
heart We, my friend, see ourselves.
A flower always grows towards the light of
the sun. Leaving the grass behind.
We do not want to
Grow for to grow,
means pain of letting
GO. But you keep
growing no matter
what.
In every direction.
A flower only grows
towards the sun.
That is the only difference between a flower
and you We have a right to be stupid, to go our
own way
But it is only through
transformation that you can
outshine even the flower. It is only
through transformation
That you can leave the grass
behind Leaving behind the pain.

*Goddess, tell me about the
world whether it will destroy
itself.*

*Close your eyes and
see it is already
happening.
We are standing on the
threshold of major disaster
We live in a world full of
aggression We live in a world
without love.
One turns his aggression towards the
world Or towards oneself.
No longer can many see their own
beauty And the beauty in the world.
Everyone wanders in all
directions Lost, lonely and
afraid.
People are killing
themselves out of fear of
seeing
what they have created.
They kill others so they
will not be killed.
It is eternal circle, going around and
around. Our creation is our reflection
it's our mirror, it's our face.
And many do not want to see the
truth. So they destroy themselves
and this beautiful world.*

But Goddess,

I don't want it be seen as the saviour of the world!

*How foolish you are
sometimes note what I say:
sometimes For sometimes
this old fear of being
condemned
that you are a preacher
man comes up in you.
But I say to you
Just start your journey of sharing in
abundance.
Only then your fear will fly
away Like a dove flying
High up to the sky The world cannot be
saved.
The world is like it is.
But one can be
awakened. One can
save oneself.*

But Goddess, people never seem to understand me.

All you have to do is understand
yourself. See your own face.
Then there is no more need for you to be
understood. Often we will do things
Hoping others will
understand us There is no
need.
By knowing
yourself you will
know others
Do not ever make any
compromises. Be yourself -
always
and a great wisdom
appears on your
horizon A knowledge
of knowing
that others never need to know
you. Everyone is special.
Do not depend on others understanding
you. Just see all there is, all that you are.
And accept this in the glory of light.

Goddess, can you tell me who I am?

*You are a blessing for the
world. And so are many
others with you. You are a
wanderer
a searcher of light
only to learn that the light lives in
you. But you had to go through
all these layers upon layers.
Fears, tears, hopes, rejections,
And the greatest: the fear of
dying. And so often Luka
the mind was in the way.
You, my friend are a very old soul
walking the earth
seeing
reflections of
your true being
everywhere.
You my friend
need to know
nothing, not
knowing is
growing.*

CONT....
It is very difficult for you
to live in such an often mad
world that consists
mostly of greed
and primitive mentality. people have not
learned why they live.
Let alone the meaning of
dying. Your light is there,
you're just one step
away from no-you.
Sometimes you take that step by
accident and then quickly step back
again
afraid to die in loving, to surrender in
no ego. You always seek the cliff,
But afraid to jump into the
ocean you run.
knowing what lies
ahead. Still you keep
searching for your lost
home
that was never lost at
all. This is the game
you play
Afraid to stand alone in your
strength A singer becomes his
song
The minute he stops
singing Then silence
answers all.

Goddess, I have such an energy to share...it frightens me!

*Your cup is running over
it is filled full of love and song and you feel the need to share. For if you don't
all that you have seen or lived
through will die forever.
Keeping it all to yourself, feels
Like breathing in a small place without ventilation
This is what happens so much to so many. People suffocate in their own abundance of love. Ventilate, my friend, your loving to the world
so others can breathe again with a fresh
breath. Flowing in love
Dancing in purity
On the river of eternal waters.*

Goddess, in your wisdom I feel so much at ease...

*You feel at ease because
You meet the woman in
you.
And women are often much more at ease. A womanly feeling makes you feel at home. A woman's wisdom is her intuition. knowing without mind.
When you hold your woman in your heart you are holding yourself.
In oneness.
In
wholeness*

Goddess, is all this not going a bit too deep?

*If there was depth I would say
yes but there is no depth
without high. One cannot exist
without the other. It always is
like this
there is no left
when there is no right. There is only truth
and truth can only be seen
through your eyes...only,
when many masks have
fallen
So that you stand naked in the
light. Like a newborn baby.
It hurts to open your eyes for the very first
time. Try it and you will see,
that after closing them for a
while and then opening them
again,
it takes a while
getting used to the light. And so it is*

when you look inside of you. S
That is why you asked me
Whether this is not going a bit too deep. Out
of fear of being hurt.
But truth can only be seen in light.
and soon as you awake in light. Your
eyes can never be hurt again.
Sometimes it hurts.

Goddess, I am beginning to realize so well that the Goddess is alive in me, silently speaking.

I am so glad, it was a long road for you with many obstacles in the way.
Now your road is smooth flowing like a running river. Silently knowing that you are the Goddess. Welcome to your home.

*Goddess, I want to live with you
forever.*

*It sounds like a
child asking his
mother never to
leave him.
It feels good, it feels very good.
But watch, observe what you are
doing. Are you really asking the
mother?
If so, do not suppress this feeling.
But realize that you are the
mother, the father and the son.
All three live in you.
It's the triangle of
being
in which the world is
created. Being one light.
One energy.
You are three
to become one.
So I will never abandon
you. Just follow the
stairway
to your own star.*

Goddess, can you tell me about artists?

We have such a misunderstanding of artists.
It is often said, that poets, painters, writers,
sculptors and many more creative people live on the edge
of going crazy.
Let us ask ourselves: what is this edge?
Sometimes a poet or a painter goes over the edge and get lost. But sometimes they come back with a diamond. Then often ordinary life becomes a hell for these people, having seen the light, having been one with existence. They miss something and a great longing for paradise brings them many tears of agony and frustration. Sometimes this longing becomes so big that they actually choose to die.
Look at Vincent van Gogh - millions of people all over the world are fascinated by his paintings today.
Vincent fell over the edge into the light time and time again.
Every stroke of his brush reflects this light.

CONT

In whatever they create, artists show us the hand of God. The world should take great care of them.
For they show us a new tomorrow, sowing the seeds of awareness for us and our children. It's so unfair.
They pass on the eternal beauty, while we treat them often so unkind.
For what a poor world we would live in, if there were no more artists. If there were no more songs to sing, no more dances to dance, no more paintings to look at, to touch our soul, our inner being.
It's their greatest gift, given to us. It's love in its purest form.
And if we realize all this, then we will see, that there is no death, no dying.
Then we will see that all creation goes on forever, existing in one form or the other.
It's the eternal spiral of existence.

Goddess, are there no more words to be said?

No, there are no more words to be said.

Before there were words, there was silence. Only silence. And only in silence, when nothing is said, truth can enter. Words are created in the mind. And they can only exist in thoughts.
Words belong to the past. Not to the moment. And it's only when one meets the moment, that truth arises.
No, for now there is nothing to be
said. For silence says it all.
Our conversation was a revelation to help you to see this by yourself, for seeing is being.
No, once again, there is nothing to be
said. All has been spoken in one way or
the other. My words are from you.

For these are not my words they are now **yours**.
And like me, live your life in silence, just listen to the song of life.
Be Silent in your silence, so you can hear the unheard

Goddess ,

I now have left your island
You gave me everything

Now I feel I have nothing.
In this nothingness, you will find everything.
Don't cling to what you have got: the house, the
motor, the car, your friends, not all of this.
For your car will get old and rusty, friends may
come and go and your home may be destroyed.
You think you own all these things and try to keep
hold on them.
But it's only when you stop clinging, that you will
find you have everything. It's always like that. Let
go of all the things you posses, that posses you, and
all is yours.
Look at the stars. They do not cling to the
sky. The beach does not cling to the sea.
Really. You will see:
You will come home when you become homeless.

*Wherever you go, you will meet
me. Whenever you want to, I will
be there. For you are.
For once you have tasted the fruits of your
Goddess, She will speak to you,
like the tree of
wisdom, a flame of
light. Beyond your
heart
lies a seed of a flower,
waiting for the rain to
shower Only when you see
the light You can blow out
the candle.*

BEING IN ALL

THERE IS NO END

NOW YOU COME OSHO SAID

BY

LUKA VAN DEN DRIESSHEN

(ALOK GAYAKA)

OSHO (BHAGWAN) 1990

This is my story

NEVER BORN

NEVER DIED

ONLY VISITED THIS PLANET EARTH BETWEEN

1931--1990

LUKA VAN DEN DRIESSCHEN

(ALOK GAYAKA)

PUNE 1989

Introduction

As I write these words, it is over 20 years (1990)ago that a plane from China Airways took me to Bombay, where a bus drove me to Pune to my beloved master Osho, who was spending his last few weeks on this earth. On my way - not knowing what was awaiting me - I opened up my heart as singer of light swami Alok Gayaka. This is my story. It is part of my autobiographic book 'Reborn') which at this moment is available also in Dutch German and even in Chinese.

As a historic moment of untold value it is a close account of a swami in love with his master, being so grateful for having heard his voice a few weeks before he went in to Samadhi: now you come ….now you come. And I came and all that happened there during that time is written down here to share with you. May it touch your heart like my heart was touched then in the year 1990, when I stood there at the burning ghat - all dressed in white – singing, while the last blocks of wood were laid down on the face of Osho: " The universe is singing a song, the universe is dancing along."

And this is my song.

Luka van den Driesschen

(Alok Gayaka)singer of light
Amersfoort 2018

WITH LOVE AND THANKS TO AMRITA

FOR THE TRANSLATION

My ship is ready-- any moment I can depart... This is not your home-- at the most an overnight stay.

My Beloved Ones, I love you. Love is my message, my color and my climate... In love you disappear, your mind disappears. In love you come to an utter relaxation. That's my teaching to you, I teach love. And there is nothing higher than love.

My trust in existence is absolute. If there is any truth in what I am saying, it will survive. The people who remain interested in my work will be simply carrying the torch but not imposing anything on anyone.

... never send to know for whom the bell tolls -- it tolls for Thee. In death, we are all equal. In life, we may be different, separate, individuals. In death, individuality, all separation, disappears.'

Everybody stands in the same queue a caravanserai... you stay for the night and by the morning you are gone.

There has always been an empty chair before you... I will be there, and if you meditate rightly, whenever your meditation is exactly tuned, you will see me. So that will be the criterion of whether you are really meditating or not. Many of you will be able to see me more intensely than you can see me right now; and whenever you see me, you can be certain that things are happening in the right direction. So this will be the criterion... And once you can feel me in my absence, you are free of me. And then, even if I am not here in this body, the contact will not be lost.

I will see through your eyes and I will talk through your tongues. And I will touch people through your hands. And I will love through your love... I am preparing for the future: A commune with one voice, one direction and one soul.

Pune (1989-1990)

Pune, INDIA

Again, I was sleeping in the special room downstairs where Jan Foudraine used to have his office. Within seven days everything was organized. I had sold a few more things to have some pocket money while traveling. Only my guitar and my recording equipment were traveling with me. My ex-wife and my girlfriend Betty took me to Schiphol airport. Within twenty four hours I would be landing at Bombay. I had heard that I was not supposed to tell anyone where I was going because of the risk to be send back immediately. Nothing in my luggage should betray the goal of my journey. Fortunately I passed the customs at Bombay without a scratch. Coming out of the airport some man approached me immediately asking where I was going. I felt and I saw right away that this man was no taxi driver but a cop. I pretended not to understand him and said 'no I don't need a taxi' which made him even angrier. And again I repeated: 'me no need no taxi, me stay in Bombay...' Finally he gave up and let go of me. And before I knew it I was in the bus heading for Pune, about 400 kilometers from Bombay.

While getting there I could not believe my eyes. What hit me were the big amounts of people but also the tremendous poverty they were living in. This was the culture shock people had warned me for. At first, I did not want to see it and I wanted to close my eyes, but still I kept on looking. We continued right through the slums of Bombay where it looked as if people were living on top of each other in small huts and tents. No, this did not make me feel very happy. In a flash I wanted to go back home with the first airplane available but practically this was not possible. I booked my return flight with a Chinese air company that would reach Bombay again one week later. My thoughts were racing..... really, everybody criticizing the West should be sent to India for a while! Another thing I had to get used to was the way the Indians continuously move their heads when talking to you – right, left, right, left. As if they apologize for everything they are saying. The bus was climbing its way through the mountains. After some time the landscape turned into green. I saw flowers everywhere and thus I regained some peace of heart. Once again I found the love inside of me, the same love that took me on this journey. The love for Osho that called me when I was in Crete: 'now you come, now you come'. Just a few kilometers and the bus would stop close to the ashram, but for now, the bus was going through the mountains passing by eerie steep abysses. As soon as I reached Pune I booked the very first hotel.

The hotel room was not a big deal. Except for a bed and a big fan rotating at the ceiling, there was nothing. Later on, I found out that I was still a few kilometers away from the ashram, so the next day I went looking for a place close by. It seemed as if Osho's energy inside of me had become stronger. Being so close to Him my heart was beating like crazy out of fear and emotion. It felt like pain as if I was dying again. 'Help me' said a tiny little voice inside of me. It was the voice of a very small boy, but nobody heard me. India with all its misery made me feel insecure made me feels scared. All a traveling of mine had not made me fireproof against so much misery and poverty. While on the streets I had to step over a dead man's body, avoid some cripple old man and get rid of children shouting at me 'you give me money, you give me money!' Did not Osho say on one occasion 'giving doesn't help them'? In that way you confirm their poverty and you keep hem small. Rather teach hem how to make money. 'But really, what do you do when you see a small child die from hunger? That child needs to eat *now*, needs somebody *now*. I myself had given up my safety and my wealth for an insecure existence but I could always go back if it were really necessary. However, they, were could they go?

The next day I found a hotel room close to the ashram, not very expensive. Now the moment had come that I myself was walking Koregaon Road, the street where the ashram was located and that I had read about in so many books. It was a long road with many stalls and sannyasins everywhere. At the end of this road was the gate that gave access to the ashram. To be allowed in one had to first show one's Aids test and pay a small amount of money. This I knew and so I had it with me. Thereupon I was allowed in and I could get myself registered. The feeling I had upon entering was overwhelming. I was speechless. It felt as if I had come home. Tears were flowing, I was deeply moved inside. Now I was really close to Osho, just a few meters separated us. I looked around and noticed how beautiful everything was here: the pond, the swans, the plants, the flowers and the enormous Buddha hall. Almost everybody was dressed in red. It was not compulsory but I decided to buy such a dress too the next day, a red one for the daytime and a white one for the nighttime. I was so blown away by the beauty, the light and the energy that I could not control myself when a female sannyasin said to me while guiding us around 'look, that' where Osho lives!' Thousands of golden tears rolled down my cheeks. Crying I moved on and my heart was singing: 'We are flowers in your garden, opening, opening….' I had been singing the same song in the bus on my way to Oregon. 'We are flowers in your garden, opening' but now it was different, essentially different. My feet were walking on clouds, stars surrounded my head, and I started to experience a unity, just one more step, a little bit further on, one stretch home. So many emotions, so many impressions, so may people from all over he world, everybody carrying that same feeling of 'we love you Osho'. It was surrealistic to watch. In my own life, Osho had had already a special place for some time, but now I saw that the whole world was touched by him or at least part of our planet. He was not only just part of me anymore. This gave me a feeling of recognition. The next morning I bought a maroon dress and a white one for the evenings in Buddha hall. With my cute white shoes, my Gazelle sunglasses, my Rolex and my diamond ring that my German girlfriend had given to me, I looked beaming and that is how I felt. While walking I was floating above the street. I had to make the biggest effort to stay grounded. It seems as if I was pulled upwards towards the light and at the same time, I went down into the abyss, my abyss, death. Like an old medieval monk in my maroon robe, I walked the lanes of the ashram. I sat down in front of the big white Buddha statue and watched it. At times, I closed my eyes and disappeared into nothing. I felt fear, I felt death. Quickly I moved and sat down somewhere else to smoke a cigarette. I had read somewhere that smoking was like burning incense for your own soul. It was only just my second day in the ashram and it hit me that there were many Germans, who occupied themselves mainly with the organization, because that is what they are good at. That night – for the first time dressed in my white robe – I was watching the crowd lining up to be 'sniffed' before they were allowed into the Buddha hall where Osho would be present that night, alive and well. I was not ready yet to enter there and sit still for three hours without being allowed to fart, cough, let alone sneeze. While I was watching all this, a beautiful young woman carrying a baby in her arms approached me. She had dark brown eyes and being so young and innocent she asked me in half German half English if I would like to be the baby's father for some time, because she had come on her own with her child all the way from Germany. I was astounded. What openness, what courage! I felt like the chosen one and before I knew what was happening I was walking through the ashram behind a buggy with a ten-month-old little boy in it. That night the celebration continued. We slept together like a real mom and dad with the baby right next to us waking up every now and then. I had to think about how my journey started, my fears and my doubts, and here she was that young woman who had made the same journey taking even her baby with her. 'Miracles do exist' I thought.

It is no secret that children were not much wanted in those days in the Bhagwan movement. A child was supposed to hinder your own growth. Osho would have said that time was running out and that we did not have one minute to lose and therefore did not have time to raise children. I could feel it from the looks we got from other sannyasins even though I was not even the real father. In addition, did not Jesus himself said: 'let thy children come to me?' My own inner child was wide-awake. I saw God reflected in the children: the purity, the oneness of the moment, the openness, and the freedom. I know that every man has to be reborn to become a child again so he can find God and allow the divine. A child lives in nothingness, in everything, in the moment. Again and again, he lets go of everything and to be able to experience oneness you have to be able to let go of everything. This is my own experience.

Overwhelmed by joy, overwhelmed by the light, but also with a dark fear of death I was walking through the ashram. I was there and yet I was not there. I do not know how to describe it otherwise. I was walking more slowly and my movements became slower because I was being more and more in the moment. One can see this happen also with the monks in a monastery. However, alongside with the stillness all the time there was this fear and I was dying inside while being in the rickshaw on my way to the ashram holding myself so I would not fly off. The deepest parts of me came to the surface again: the fear of drowning, the fear of death. I was dying again but this time between beautiful people who told me, I looked beautiful. I remember thinking 'how is this possible, I am dying!'

One time I was standing at the river with the mother and her little boy. She put her arm around me and said softly 'just one more little step, Alok, then you will be home again'. But really, who dares to take that little step? You are drowning, you are dying. I had been screaming all those years 'I'm dying' and nobody understood me and they had put me in jails and madhouses. And now I had to die again... While being so much afraid of dying I was hearing music, lyrics and songs in my head even more strongly than before. It would not stop and every time I was running to my hotel room to write them down, one song after another.

One night I was standing in line again at the Buddha hall waiting to be sniffed. They almost didn't let me in because they could still smell my smoking habits even though I rubbed myself with lots of scentless soap The mother of the baby apologized for me saying 'it is his first time, he just arrived'. Then somebody pushed me on the back meaning I could move on. All of a sudden I was standing there with thousands of other people in the big Buddha hall. I stayed at the back of the hall with all these fears rushing through me. All of a sudden Osho appeared on stage. After giving away some energy in the way only he can do he sat down on a chair. I saw him slipping of one of his sandals like I had seen him do on so many videos before. I was there just watching it all. I saw a tiny man in the distance but his light filled me with a tremendous feeling of joy and gave me so much strength and love. I was taken away riding on the waves of pure being. I was drinking heavenly nectar, yes I became drunk of this heavenly nectar, really, how is this possible? But it happened! Afterwards I left the Buddha hall. It seemed I was floating and my feet did not touch the earth. Next to me a ma was walking, she was German also, and just like that, we walked together to a stall where they sold crystals. I picked one that carried a lot of power. That ma, whom I will call Deva here, was working herself with crystals a lot. She proposed to me to go to my hotel room – or maybe I did, I do not remember – but some moments later, we were lying on the bed naked, drunk with love with the crystal on top of her, then on top of me. The love was so intense that the bed - big and heavy - had flown from one side of the room to the other side by the enormous power. Because of this intense experience in the Buddha hall, I did not dare to enter Buddha hall again fearing I would never be my old self again. I was afraid I would just vanish from the earth. When one day I was meditating on a little brick wall, I saw Jan Foudraine walking just close by. I ran towards him to greet him. I wanted to hug him like old comrades do but somehow he let me know that he did not like this at all and continued walking. I watched how he walked over to another wall and sat there. I could not accept his reaction, walked towards him again, and sat down next to him. He snapped at me: 'I'm talking to someone else right now'. I was thunderstruck. There he was right next to me that man for whom I had strained myself for all those years. Many had called him 'an arrogant son-of-a -bitch' and now I started to believe this myself. Every evening I was standing along the road waiting for Osho to drive in his Rolls Royce from his home to the Buddha hall. Each time he arrived, I could see his headlights lightning up in the dark. The fairy-like green lanterns hanging in the plants and trees created a very mystical atmosphere. My heart was throbbing but strangely enough my feet did not want to go into the Buddha hall after seeing Osho but they walked by themselves as it were through the gate, outside onto the streets towards the river, towards the burning Ghats were they cremated the dead. There I sat all by myself in the dark on a bench, dying in silence. Fully surrendered I lost my fear of death and a feeling of total relaxation descended on me, as if I finally came home with singing voices or Osho's voice talking on the video in the distance. In those days, he himself did not talk anymore in public. I did not understand myself why I was doing this but this ritual repeated itself night after night. Again and again, I came back to that same spot, just naturally. Later on, I discussed this with Jan Foudraine, but he thought I was ego tripping and actually needed therapy for it. For me it was something totally different. I did not dare to enter the Buddha hall because I was afraid to go completely crazy or I would die. And my heart kept on screaming: 'I'm dying'. That fear of dying, that damned fear of dying while you are alive, can it be a natural phenomenon?

I had brought my beautiful Ovation guitar with me and also my own recording equipment and microphones just in case. Between the bushes and the flowers I found myself a place somewhat away from it all and for the first time I started to sing the songs I had written there: In the night I saw the light'..Tell me where is heaven...if the earth turns around.' One day somebody sat down next me and asked me to join for a concert and I said 'yes!' right away. After some rehearsing, I found myself on the stage of the big concert hall singing together with other people accompanied by an orchestra or accompanying myself on the guitar. For a moment I thought they did not like it and they were going to throw tomatoes at me bit it turned out to be roses... With all my heart I sang this famous song of Elvis Presley 'Can't help falling in love'. And while I was singing that song and my voice was echoing through the bamboo groves I saw in my mind Osho sitting in his home in his chair just half a mile away and my heart said: 'this song is for you.'

I remember sitting somewhere outside the ashram on a little terrace meeting a ma sannyasin whom I knew from Holland, where she had on Osho centre not far away from my hometown. When she recognized me, she said 'O God, if you are here in Pune, something is bound to happen. You don't just come here. 'Then I told her that Osho had called me when

I was on the isle of Crete. At that moment, we suddenly heard a loud explosion not far away from us as if lightning had struck nearby. We both jumped. It turned out that a big monkey had jumped from a tree onto an electricity cable, had been electrocuted and fell down. We were both totally upset. 'Yes' I can still hear her say, 'a lot is going to happen, Alok, it is already happening.' She did not say anything else. Right after this, I heard that Vivek, Osho's companion, had committed suicide and had been cremated in silence. Yes, death was already around. Also that beautiful ma with her little child whom I had come to know was one day just walking outside the ashram territory and people were throwing stones at her. Fortunately, it all ended well, but I started to hear these stories around me more and more.

One evening I went with my friend from Berlin with whom I had spent that 'crystal night' to the burning Ghats. While sitting there on a bench near the river we heard the sounds of the Buddha hall in the distance. Then she wanted to play the guitar and sing some song. I kept the microphone ready and while she was singing, we heard somebody screaming and shouting coming our way. A man approached us with a big stone in his hand ready to hit us on the head. On the verge of death, my friend put down the guitar and with folded hands made the gesture of 'Namaste', which means: I salute the light in you. And, as if a miracle happened, the man put down the stone right there and then.

Some other day I was eating in my hotel room when somebody knocked at the door. A female sannyasin from Australia came to thank me that I had cured her with my songs and she strongly advised me to do something with this gift of mine. She came from Tasmania and told me

she was a doctor in literature. I still remember thinking: yet another woman who had come to India by herself feeling she had been called.

One day Jan Foudraine came up to me (this time he did!) and asked me if I wanted to read the manuscript of a small booklet that he wrote. I could take it to my hotel and bring it back after a couple of days. I could not wait and went to my hotel right away to read it. Already after a few hours I had finished it. I took the manuscript back to the ashram and approached Jan. He could not believe I had already read it all. After I told him what it was about he asked me 'and, what do you think?' 'I miss your feeling' I said, 'Jan'. The next day I saw him writing while seated at a big table in the sun. Without saying anything, I brought him a cup of coffee and a cookie and walked away without saying anything. I loved that man so much, so very much. He wanted the whole of Holland to walk around in red clothes. He wanted to share his diamond with everybody, at no matter what price he himself and others had to pay for it. Just like me, yes, just like me. 'Thank you' I still heard him say in the distance. I turned around for a second and nodded. I sat down in another part of the ashram, took my guitar and started to sing'...sitting in your garden of love in your new creation, seeing all the people from all nations...being love, being one sound...going around and around.' Singing in the ashram became a daily ritual. I did not join any groups, because I thought I had been in therapy enough during my lifetime. However, I did sit in the beautiful garden in front of the Buddha statue regularly and turned inside. Sometimes when I was sitting there this old fear of dying came up again. By holding on to the fear nothing new can be born. Only by taking some distance from it and letting go of it the old will die and give space to what is new. To die is to be born again. It is all about surrender like life itself is surrendering to yourself. In marriage you surrender to the other who is a mirror for your true face. My fire had been stirred up and holy smoke was on its way. One of my most beautiful memories concerns the

comments of a beautiful ma from Germany. She said, 'you are afraid of your own power! Every time you fall back into the past, you become that little boy again and you become afraid of what and whom you really are. Because really, you are a guy with so much power that you become afraid of it yourself.'

I had never heard something like that before. It was a totally different approach than the endless moldings of your past through regression therapy of which I had absolutely had my fill. 'Das ist alles was ich zu sagen habe' she said. Then something happened to me. I got up, walked away, and felt an enormous strength in my legs and in my belly and then in my whole body, it was unheard of. A few moments later that little boy came up again and then that strength again. That experience never left me. It brought about a great turnaround in my life and I am still grateful to her for this insight. Every time I said to myself, 'you are afraid of your power' and that did work. It was one of the biggest gifts in my life and was it not a simple one? It was time for the Zorba, the stallion in me. It was going to be this strength that later on in my life many times proved to be very valuable.

In the ashram I also met an Indian doctor who lived in Holland in the first Bhagwan centre, where I also used to come in the beginning. He was one of the first who had come to Osho, already in the early days. Sometimes when I looked at him, I felt he was enlightened but he himself did not mention this at all. One night while drinking something together in a restaurant, I saw a certain look in his eyes and I knew he had reached somewhere. His way of life was 'to do nothing' and like Osho had said 'letting the grass grow by itself.' And I remembered again how he got up late in the morning, walked around with only a small towel wrapped around his waist and took a long shower while the others in the centre were *worship-ping*. Then I heard the other people who were working

hard say: 'his way is to do nothing'. One does not easily forget a scene like that and I remember thinking at the time; I would like to have a small towel wrapped around myself too!

Weeks were passing by quickly. Within a few weeks I would fly back to Holland. Nevertheless, I fell ill, seriously ill. I was dying in fear of death. I felt weak and had no more the strength to get up. The owner of the hotel where I stayed turned out to be a doctor too, but he did not know what was wrong with me. I was lying in my hotel room on a big double bed while the electric fan was spinning above me and my life started to unroll itself like a movie in front of my eyes. Everything that I had experienced in the past I saw appearing repeatedly in front of me. For days, I was lying there, very much weakened and almost petrified. Nobody visited me and I did not want to eat anything, only some liquid. I accepted that my death was coming, because I knew what it meant when your life started to unravel itself to you like that. I must have laid there for five days or so, I do not remember exactly. Then a moment came that my body filled itself with power. My arms and my legs became powerful and strong again. I remember getting up at around six in the evening and I thought I should go out and eat and drink something in the ashram. I went out onto the street and a rickshaw took me to a small restaurant where I had eaten before. Usually it was full of sannyasins but this time I was sitting all by myself on the terrace. I ordered a plate of rice and a cola. I took only some rice because I had not eaten for a while and felt I had not landed on the earth yet. After sitting there for just a few minutes, the waiter came up to me and said: 'Don't you know that Osho has died?' 'Yes, yes' I said because I thought he was kidding me. Quietly I ate my rice and finished my cola. I was still sitting just by myself on the terrace when a young woman dressed in red came up to me, stopped her bicycle in front of me and yelled 'Osho has died! Osho has died!' and we should all come to Buddha hall at seven dressed in white. I

almost fell backwards I was swept away and felt an enormous upsurge of energy going to my head. She saw what happened to me and I heard her yell at me 'feel your heart, swami, feel your heart'. All of a sudden I felt an unknown force rising up inside of me. Quickly I paid to the waiter, jumped into a rickshaw and went back to my hotel. The hotel manager by then had also heard that Osho had died. I remember still that he asked me - because I was the only sannyasin still there - whether this would be the end of the ashram and therefore his hotel. I answered him that this was only the beginning and that now even more people would be coming to Pune, which was really reassuring to him. I went inside quickly and put on my white robe. After this I hurried to the ashram. When I arrived there, everything looked upside down. Everywhere in the Buddha hall there were clothes and shoes. The people were standing there with disbelief on their face, some of them were crying. This time nobody sniffed us when entering the Buddha hall and just as well because I had nervously been smoking a lot. Still there was peace and no panic. I settled myself in the back and to my surprise, only few people had shown up. Later on, I heard that many had not heard the news yet and were just dining somewhere or had left to Goa for a few days. Everybody was waiting for an official announcement from Osho's personal physician. I felt strong and quietly waited for what was to come. I did not feel any grief, at least not yet, and I noticed many others did not either. I remembered that Osho had said many times that there was a negative energy in the Buddha hall because certain people did things that were not ok. Was it because of this that I did not dare to enter the Buddha hall? Would it have caused Osho's death? I remember what the wife of this Dutch doctor had told me: 'If you are here in Pune something is going to happen. You don't just come here', I still heard her say. In addition, I heard Osho's voice again calling me at Crete: 'Now you come; now you come.' In addition, here I was at this very important moment in history. Osho had died and his body would soon go up in flames: '...a burning fire, turning all around...'

And there we were waiting for Osho to be carried inside. And that which had been told to us before did happen. Osho's body was being carried inside on a sort of stretcher surrounded by flowers and put on the stage. I was standing on tiptoe and stared at my master whom I had loved so much, together with so many others. Feelings of joy, sadness and relief wee taking possession of me with an unknown force and intensity. Had he not said himself 'kill your master'? And now he was dead himself or rather putting it this way: he had left his body. But what about this feeling of relief, which I thought I noticed in others also, where did this come from? Once Osho himself had said 'If I am no longer in the body I will follow you into every nook and corner of the world.' In fact, it would be easier for him to follow us while dead than alive. In the speech that followed, they announced that Osho's body would be burnt in the evening of that very same day. At around eight, they would take his body to the burning Ghats. They also told us how he had died. His private doctor, Amrito, appeared on the stage and told us that Osho had died from heart failure and that he had distributed his last personal belongings between a few close disciples. Around 20.00 hrs we all came together outside the gate. At some distance, I saw Jan Foudraine finding his way all by himself. I heard my friend Atma say 'I am going to get a drink, he is anyway not in his body anymore.' I remember thinking: 'How can you say a thing like that', but I did not have much time to think about it. I joined the procession that was formed by around one thousand people. At the beginning of the procession, the stretcher with Osho's body on it was being carried. Osho's last journey went through the streets of Pune towards the burning Ghats. It all looked very unreal. We were walking in the middle of the streets while the busy traffic was rushing alongside of us. I noticed many inhabitants standing at the side of the road looking totally surprised. Suddenly one part of the procession went off into a totally different direction. I never found out why. All of a sudden, I was walking right behind Osho's body. I experienced it as if I was walking behind his dead body all by myself. It looked like a fair, heaven and hell simultaneously in the middle of all this traffic noise. The heat of the night was suffocating me. I did not understand were all these thousands of sannyasins had gone who had still been there in the ashram during the day. Once at the burning Ghats Osho was transferred to one of the spots where bodies are being burned, a few meters from where I had been recording the week before. I myself did not want to stand in the front row. Together with maybe one thousand (or more) other people I was looking from some distance how other people arranged logs of wood around Osho while we were singing in the darkness of the night: 'the universe is singing a song, the universe is dancing along, the universe is singing on a day like this. 'We kept repeating only this one song all the time. One sannyasin, a German therapist, came standing next to me. I put my arm around her to give her energy. After this had happened, I gave her a little push as if I was saying 'now you have to continue by yourself'. A few moments later I saw her dancing and singing. The whole burning ghat was now full of sannyasins. I looked over the crowd and saw how the last logs of wood were being put on top of Osho. Only his face remained visible. When I looked again I saw that now this last part had been covered with wood also. This was the last I saw of Osho. That image that very last moment, always stayed with me. Slowly everything was getting on fire now. Clouds of smoke went up in the air. Here he went, our master. Time was standing still and we all stood there thunderstruck. This went deep, very deep. An unreal silence prevailed and a quietness from which arose a certain grace, call it love, and it filled my heart and everybody else's also. The flames became more and more intense and the smell of fire and smoke reached my nostrils and hid itself in the white robe I was wearing. 'Goodbye master', my heart was saying, 'goodbye biggest one of this earth, this is the second time I'm with you, now that you are leaving your body. Thank you for everything you gave to me, that you called me at Crete so I could be here this moment' and my heart was singing: ' ...the universe is singing a song, the universe is dancing along...'

And while everybody was singing and dancing Osho's body burnt until only some smoldering ashes of bones and wood remained. However, in the darkness of the night a light had been lit in my heart, a great light. With that experience in my heart I walked back towards the ashram. On the way I passed crying and stunned sannyasins who had just heard what had happened and could not understand it yet. They just returned from their evening dinner or from a two-day trip to Goethe were sitting under a tree in dismay trying to come to terms with their sadness. I was crying too, but my tears were tears of gratitude. By now it was midnight. Stars were twinkling in the sky and I heard Osho say 'I'll be where Jesus is, Buddha, Krishna and so many others.... And I leave you my dream.'

I was walking back to the ashram through the dark night under a sky with stars shining brightly. I felt enlightenment, or was it relief? At the big gate of the ashram there was nobody to check you this time. The whole ashram was almost deserted, only clothes and shoes were lying around here and there in the Buddha hall. For a moment I walked over to the vegetarian restaurant. The food was standing there in big bowls waiting for its customers. Also in the shop where Osho's books and videos are sold it was quiet. Looking through the window pushing my nose against the glass, I became once more aware of the treasure Osho had left us with. They say he wrote 600 books. Suddenly I burst out in tears: tears of gratitude, of sadness, of being moved so much. I looked inside again and saw a few posters and at that moment, I felt that Osho was not dead but alive like he had never lived before, free from the earth, free from his body that had caused him so much pain. In my heart I saw him smiling with that well-known smile of his, his hands folded in the Namaste gesture saying: I greet the light inside of you.

Then my eyes fell on book with the title 'Socrates poisoned again' showing a picture of Osho at Crete on its cover. Crete where the government ordered him to leave he island as soon as possible threatening to blow up the villa where he stayed would he refuse. Seeing that picture and that book I was screaming: 'they can't do that, Osho, send you away. I promise you I go back to Greece, to Crete as your 'singer of light', the name that you gave to me. Being your sannyasin I will sing my heart out.' Suddenly I felt an upsurge of energy and tears kept coming. 'Alok Gayaka' I heard a soft voice, 'Alok Gayaka, singer of light.' Never before that name seemed to suit me so much. Because when I got that name and I told Amrito Jan Foudraine proudly about my new name, he just said 'you are not your name!' Saying this he created a lot of confusion inside of me. But his voice had slowly disappeared and a new strength came in its place, a strength of light and 'the right to be myself'.

I ordered some food and went to sit at a table under the trees. With every bite I looked up and thought 'somewhere up there must be Osho, and Jesus and Buddha and so many more enlightened souls.'

After I finished eating, I got up and noticed that my feet were very light. Step by step I moved out of the ashram and called a rickshaw that took me back o my hotel. That night I suddenly woke up again. It is hard to describe what happened exactly but a song came falling down as it were from heaven descending upon me. Because I did not want to forget it, I quickly grabbed my DAT-recorder and my guitar and recorded the song.

The song almost did not have any words in it just 'shalalala, shalaaaaaaa, a Buddha is born again.' It kept on repeating itself, higher and higher all the time. It happened to me before that while writing poems my pen would just move by itself. But this went beyond all imagination. It was like soft lightning striking. I did not understand any of it. But some things you cannot understand. Some things you should not even *want* to understand.

The next morning I woke up early. Again I took a risk that brought me back to the ashram. Once I got there, there was a big silence all around. Something was missing. Something had gone and hat something was Osho. A few photographers and television people were still walking around. Maybe they were waiting for something sensational. Maybe they thought that we would collectively commit suicide, but that did not happen. On the contrary! A serene peacefulness prevailed. It seemed there was a feeling of relief now that Osho had left his body. Did not he himself had said 'Kill your master' as the last step towards enlightenment? He had even said that he could be closer to us once he had left his body. I will dissolve into all my sannyasins, because they are the slat of the earth. That day I heard that Osho's ashes would be collected and put into a pot and that they would carry that pot in procession back to the ashram. There the urn would be placed in a beautiful room with a stone next to it saying: "Osho never born, never died' and the date. When the procession passed by, I was standing together with thousands of other sannyasins along the road with a bag full of rose flowers. Osho's brother in the procession was carrying the copper urn on his shoulder. The moment he passed the bystanders threw the rose flowers towards the urn. Suddenly the procession came to a halt. That very moment the copper urn was less than half a meter away from me. My eyes were staring at the pot that carried the remains of my master. A little clumsily, I threw some rose flowers towards the urn also. Right that moment a few German sannyasins whom I had met before were walking behind me. One of them yelled at me 'Now you dare to enter Buddha hall don't you, now Osho is not here anymore.' I thought this was a mean thing to say at the wrong time. I had always followed my own path and never moved with the masses. But also I had died, although I was not really aware of it then. I did realize this was a very big happening. The procession moved on again and slowly Osho's urn on his brother's shoulder disappeared in the distance towards the ashram. Most of the sannyasins followed the procession to the ashram. I promised myself too that I would return one day to the place were Osho is buried. But when this would be, I did not know, because in a few days I would fly back to Holland. Before this, I had to do something important. I went back to the burning Ghats. I felt a strong urge to take something from what was left of Osho's body at the burning ghats. I felt I was not allowed to take any of the burning remains with my bare hands. Therefore, I took some tissues with me from a restaurant along the way. After arriving at the burning ghats I took the tissues in my hand and without giving it any further thought I picked something up that looked like a small piece of skull. After this, I folded the tissue with all respect and put it carefully in my pocket without touching it or looking at it. It was too holy for me. With this piece of bone I had a relic that would travel back with me to Holland.

That night Osho's personal physician appeared in the Buddha hall and reported what had happened exactly and how Osho had left his body. He mentioned heart failure, a conscious death, but I was questioning this. Had he been murdered or poisoned with thallium, who can tell? What did impress me very much were Osho's last words: 'I leave you my dream.' and while Amrito was talking I heard a rooster crow at this very unusual hour. This time neither I had entered the Buddha hall, but I was sitting outside watching and listening surrounded by the bamboo groves.

A few meters away from me, some other people were sitting and I remember some huge negative energy coming my way. It scared me to death and I wanted to run away. Was this what Osho had tried to point out to us just before he died? That there were people with a terrible negative energy who visited the ashram night after night? Were those people the people Osho was referring to just before he went into Samadhi (left his body?)? I suddenly remembered the lectures by Jan Foudraine, where often on the first row people were sitting with crosses on their chest to conjure him and how I stayed close to him during the interval because I was afraid they would kill him. That same negative charge and even a thousand times stronger I felt now in the ashram. Osho's death, my death, everything had died. That night I switched on my recorder again, picked up my guitar and recorded the song that was coming through me: 'I leave you my dream. 'Those were Osho's last words. It is the title of the very song that thousands of people all over the world are downloading from my website right now. Who could have imagined in 1990 that this would happen? Those last days before leaving I was playing my songs as usual out in the open in the ashram, in the smoking temple. When I sang this song 'I leave you my dream' for the first time an Indian looking man came up to me with tears in his eyes. He kneeled down before me and said 'What can I give to you?' and as if I were God himself I answered 'Your tears are enough'. He looked into my eyes, got up worthily like a prince, and walked away. I felt I had found my destination. I had gone further than even death could take me. My feet could hardly touch the earth anymore. The light of pure being had absorbed me. My heart had become even more open. I had always followed my own footsteps and now I felt that the time had come to return to Holland. That night I had dinner one more time with friends in a beautiful restaurant surrounded by plants and trees. While we were eating, I was boasting that I wanted to start a village on the isle of Santorini in Greece, whereupon my dinner mates yelled 'Sure, let us know when you're ready!' It felt really as if a voice inside of me called me to start a village. At first I thought I had gone mad, but later on it did not feel so alien after all. Santorini was my home base. The beauty and the energy of this island had brought enlightenment to many. Now it was time to say goodbye. As a farewell present, I gave to the Australian woman next door a cassette with some songs of the life recordings at the burning Ghats. She was notably happy with it and said 'this is historic document, take good care of it.' 'Yes', I said softly, 'I will'. After this, I said goodbye to her and all my other friends. Some moments later, I sat in a taxi on my way to the airport and that night I arrived at Bombay airport intoxicated by a feeling of well being and happiness. 'Goodbye India', goodbye Osho's ashes, one day I will return again to meditate next to you in that hall, one day...but I do not know when.'

> Life is his gift,
> death is his gift;
> the body is his gift,
> the soul is his gift.
> We celebrate everything.

ALOK GAYAKA (singer of light)2018
Luka van den Driesschen

WWW.LUKAVANDENDRIESSCHEN.COM

THE SONGS I WROTE IN INDIA CAN
BE FOUND ON YOUTUBE OR CD BABY
AMAZONE ITUNES EC.
UNDER LIFE ON THE BURNING GHAT
BY
LUKA VAN DEN DRIESSCHEN.

Osho (Bhagwan)

www.ingramcontent.com/pod-product-compliance
Lightning Source LLC
Chambersburg PA
CBHW070727160426
43192CB00009B/1350